Seasons of the Soul

Transitions and Shifts of Life

Seasons of the Soul

Transitions and Shifts of Life

Hearts Calling Publishing

Maureen Kwiat Meshenberg

Oak Park, Illinois

©2014

Seasons of the Soul: Transitions and Shifts of Life

© 2009-2014 by Maureen Kwiat Meshenberg

Books may be purchased in quantity and/or special sales by contacting the publisher, Hearts Calling Publishing, at 517 S Highland Avenue, Oak Park, IL 60304 | 1-773-531-7330 | or by email at Maureen@heartscallingpoetry.com

Published by: Hearts Calling Publishing
Oak Park, IL

Interior Design(s) by:
 Dylan Meshenberg (Oak Park, IL) V
 Voices in Print (Chandler, AZ);
Cover Design by: Josiah Neniskis
Editing by: Voices in Print

Creative Consultant: Anna Weber | Literary Strategist

ISBN: 978-0-9909897-0-7
10 9 8 7 6 5 4 3 2 1
1. Poetry 2. Seasons
First Edition
Printed in United States of America

Advance Praises

"Seasons of the Soul" is a beautiful book.

The raw honesty and "cracked open-ness" of Maureen Kwiat Meshenberg's poetry complements the gentle wonder in her soul, resulting in a delicacy—almost a fragility—of structure, that becomes the vessel for profound substance.

Maureen's poetry is not to be rushed. She has a very distinctive style, with what appears at times to be a superfluity of punctuation. This is not the result of haphazard sprinkling, however, but rather is a careful measuring of the pace of each piece—and every pause matters.

Reading these poems is choreography of sound and silence, light and darkness. The four seasons, spun into a tapestry of words.

~Ruth Calder Murphy
Artist and Poetess
Author of "Spirit Song", "Wings of a Thousand Tigers" and "The Dance" series of collected poetry.

The exquisite word wisdom found in *"Seasons of the Soul"* offers you comfort and delight on any sacred pilgrimage, within or without. Maureen Kwiat Meshenberg's pen to paper connects heaven and earth in this "must read and must keep" book because she knows at her soul-DNA about life's transitions. It's a companion guide to cherish on any journey and read often as I already do!

~Lore Raymond Creator, Divine Dialogue Writing
& Chief Inspirator, Women as Visionaries

Maureen's poetry is like a healing balm for the wounded heart and soul. In this compelling, awe-inspiring, hope-filled book, Maureen speaks directly to our souls. *"Seasons of the Soul"* bypasses the need the mind would have to figure out what it is reading, and instead transforms the heart in such away that one cannot help but feel peace, joy, and love, but most importantly, a knowing that winter always turns to spring.

~Jackie Barros VancCampen
Author, "Letters to My Daughter: A
Mother's Journey of Healing and
Transformation"
"Wise Heart Archetypes: The 7 levels of
Awakening the Wisdom Within" eBook
"Anthology-Miracles, Momentum, and
Manifestation – Unleash the Secret Powers
of Having the Life You Desire"
Owner and Founder | Wise Heart

"In times when my day is a scramble and I forget my center, I can read one of Maureen Kwiat Meshenberg's poems and it's puts me right where my mind needs to be! In *"Seasons of the Soul"* sometimes it brings me gratitude, there times it's letting go, or just simply allowing myself to feel all the things I'm feeling without shame or guilt but rather honoring it."

~Gina Leigh
Singer and Song Writer
Founder | The Real Jersey Girls

"Poetic kisses on a page, is how I would describe "*Seasons of the soul*". Maureen's words never fail to captivate and transport me to the place she is describing. I am always moved by her poetic food for thought, that never forces the issue at hand. "*Seasons of the soul*" is a gentle reminder that there is so much more to LIFE!!

~**Andrea Smith**
Bionic Butterfly or Bionic B
Writer/Poet & Founder of the ARTCOLAB
WINDOWS Grenada Project.

Dedication

I DEDICATE THIS book to my three amazing children for loving me through all the shifts and changes of life and accepting me for who I am. They have braved through the many changes of me and I hold each of them as precious gems of my heart.

I also dedicate this book to all the she-heroes in my life: my twin sister Marianne, my confidants and my closest friends. Without them, going through my shifts alone, would have been unbearable. They are the connection of love and life I have to this world for which I am truly grateful.

I dedicate this book to all the readers who have followed my poetry through Heart's Calling, and lovingly supported me through my publishing journey. May this book touch your hearts and souls.

I also offer this book to the Divine One who lives within me, giving me this amazing gift of poetry to share with the world.

Transitions of Me

transitions of me,
the movement of me-
standing on the changes,
that often erupt my-
world of being.
what shifts and makes me,
take pause-
what actions ,
of courage,
of faith,
of love,
can bring me to-
the emerging of my,
rising.
the seasons of my soul,
we come to our-
dying,
breathing,
birthing,

even in the shattering-
of all that was.
what brings me to,
my passage-
my chrysalis breaking,
to flying-
up above my,
minds holding-
onto what,
I believe to be secure-
all falls beneath me-
like leaves off,
an autumn tree,
my winter of me-
is now ending,
I can come out now,
and be me.

Table of Contents

Foreword

*"I believe that there is a subtle
magnetism in Nature, which,
if we unconsciously yield to it, will direct
us aright."*

~Henry David Thoreau

TUCKED INTO THE beautiful poems of
this book is the illuminating narrative of a
soul in an intimate dance with nature, as she
discovers, explores and honors herself amidst
life's transforming turns. This poetic offering
rises like a sun on the dark dawn of the
environmental crisis, reminding us of the
incredible healing power we can all summon,
in answering Mother Earth's clarion call: a
call that reflects the call of our own souls. In
her debut poetry collection, Maureen Kwiat
Meshenberg not only responds to this call,
but also invites us to accompany her as she
reaches all the wonderful places it takes her.

From rejuvenating winter and rebirthing
spring, through the color bursts of summer
and the inward pull of autumn—the author's
favorite season—we are ferried through a

poetic river of human experience, as Maureen makes compassion a golden thread she weaves throughout every seasonal shift of her soul. Fueled with this healing component, the book overflows with attractive invitations to open, receive, and allow oneself to be deeply touched by life.

"Seasons of The Soul" embraces life's most defining characteristic: that of change. Drawing from the inextinguishable nature of the soul, while old perspectives of herself and her life go up in flames, Maureen's poetry treats us to the blossoming of a voice rooted in spirit. A voice I was privileged to watch bloom, one petal at a time, as she began releasing it into the world.

I first came upon Maureen's poetry in what appeared to be a spring cycle of her creativity. Drawing deeply from treasures she had excavated during her heart's hibernation, poetry burst from Maureen like wildflowers in a field. It was July of 2013, and Maureen became one of the most active participants in the *Journey of the Heart* poetry project I was hosting. While it was most remarkable to be on the receiving end of such a flow of vibrant poetic expression, what especially struck me was Maureen's graceful ability to process life's shadows and tragedy through the power and beauty of her poetry.

We see Maureen's gift for communicating difficult subjects in relatable ways skillfully unfold upon the pages, as her words massage the reader's heart. A generous voice for those who have yet to find theirs, the poetry in this collection echoes journeys many of us will recognize, paths we feel we have walked upon, rivers we nearly drowned in while swimming across. In sharing the familiar without reservation, Maureen becomes another pioneer in a new lineage of contemporary women poets inviting readers to rediscover themselves, and, as American poet Louise Bogan once said: "…give back to the world, through her work, a portion of its lost heart"

Catherine Ghosh
Editor, "Journey of the Heart: Spiritual Poetry by Women"
womenspiritualpoetry.blogspot.com

Acknowledgement

Josiah David Neniskis

IT IS WITH amazing awe and love for his talent that I introduce to you the young artist

who designed the stunning cover for "Seasons of the Soul," Josiah David Neniskis. I came to a place of searching, seeking, wanting and waiting... and found his remarkable piece calling to me. This piece reveals many aspects of my book: the kinship with the moon and stars, the alluring blue water touching earth, and flowers and leaves gracing her with delicate tenderness; the seasons of my soul in her eyes. With a resounding yes, I knew this would be the cover for my book. I extend my deepest gratitude to Josiah for allowing me to use this magnificent piece to represent my poetry.

Josiah David Neniskis is a Chicago born artist, influenced by comics and street-art, combined with the classical styles of oil painting. He uses symbolism and metaphors to provoke thought in his viewers about life, politics, and culture. Mostly a self-taught artist who is currently studying in school to further his abilities, he is to be applauded for raising two beautiful daughters. The blending of different styles and media gives Josiah's artwork a unique touch and feel to each piece.

Visit www.josiahdavid.com for portfolios, contact, and gallery showings.

Maureen Kwiat Meshenberg

Acknowledgement

Dylan Meshenberg

IT IS WITH great pride and joy I introduce to you the artist who is creating the trees that speak of their season my son, Dylan James Meshenberg.

Another rising talent, he will be gracing the pages of my book with his intricate and detailed beauty with a single tree representing each season. Each tree reveals delicate and individual transitions of life.

As the tree is to root and root is to earth, I identify with the growth and beauty of what the tree beholds in each season. It is with my deepest appreciation for his dedication and artistic passion that I am truly grateful his artistic tale will be illustrated in my book.

Dylan Meshenberg has always had a passion for art. In his youth he would be invited to illustrate and design programs for musical events in grade school. He continued to show his talent in High School, creating a T-shirt design for graphics design business class. The design was so successful it exceeded the sale requirements of the class. Dylan's art- work continued to be valued at art showings and shown through the walls of Oak Park River Forest High School.

During his summers in High School, Dylan participated in classes at the Art Institute of Chicago, broadening his skills and bringing him to appreciate all forms of art. Embracing the form he appreciates most is surrealism, Dylan's plans are to keep succeeding in his art career and to attend Columbia University for graphic design in the fall of 2015. The young artist currently maintains a Facebook page entitled "Toxic Artist."

(https://www.facebook.com/pages/Toxic/2 33334621073383)

About the Author

Maureen Kwiat (Meshenberg)

THIS BEAUTIFULLY PROLIFIC poet, Maureen is guided by her inner soul's journey and her warm and empathic musings about life. It was as a teenager that Maureen first started writing her unique style poetry... as a means to find her spiritual connection in her human experience. Maureen was always drawn to writing reflective soulful thoughts of the heart, bringing the shifts in life's journey to her poetry.

Her latest call to writing came after the devastating end to her 20-year marriage. The event broke her wide open—bringing forth words not only to heal herself but for many others who would read her words and find them inspiring and encouraging. The Poet's passion for writing draws her to write about life's experiences... believing we are all collectively a part of life's journey.

Her most recent work has opened many opportunities to publish on different writing blogs and online magazines, including her own Facebook page/blog called Heart's Calling, where she currently reaches almost 3,000 regular readers. Maureen presently writes for Women as Visionaries with Lore Raymond Magazine as the publication's Visionary Poet. She also writes for Journey of the Heart Blog, from which seven poems were recently selected to be published in an August, 2014 Anthology of poetesses called: *Journey of the Heart: An Anthology of Spiritual Poetry by Women.* She delivers her poetry in "spoken word" at different Chicago venues and has several publishing projects on her plate. The budding Poet is slated to have two additional poems she specifically wrote for The Art Colab Grenada Windows project to be released this October, where her unique style poetry will be viewed collectively with art in a gallery showing.

Maureen is collaborating with Bellissima Opera, a writing project to benefit inner city students in Chicago. The undertaking is a collection of the students' works of prose and poetry and developing an opera to their words. Currently hosting a Creative Writing Circle for women to utilize prose as a means of inner releasing, Maureen's words represent that raw, true reflection of her inner struggles and triumphs in life... they penetrate the hearts of those who read them—identifying with her poetry through their own struggles and triumphs.

Introduction

LIFE BELONGS TO us. It belongs to us when we hear the birds singing in the morning on a beautiful spring day. It belongs to us when we cry behind closed doors, with an ache in our soul, for whatever obstacle or pain we encounter. It belongs to us as it bends and breaks, when it moves us to our passion and we are driven to hold it all in our hearts. I hold mine in my poetry.

I write because it is my passion that stirs my desire towards life. It appears in all of my life's belonging. I write as my inner soul cries, laughs, dreams, aspires to face my journey with fierce determination and with a quiet calm of breath. My poetry is my consciousness spiraling outward in words to touch the hearts that have experience life's belonging. All of it comes to me, as I live my life, and it is with this life I share my words with you.

Seasons of The Soul are my words bringing forth the shifts and transitions of life. My poems come to me through my dying to myself and rebirthing, and it does so again and again, just like the seasons. As the seasons touch my soul with their magnificent transitions, I am moved to allegorize their journey with mine. As I identify with each season, I also feel that the season of your soul doesn't always necessarily align with how the seasons themselves transition. Your winter may be in summer; your spring in the fall.

It all has to do with your life's belonging and what is brought to your path at any given time. We never know what will come across our path... whether blue skies or a raging storm. All I know is that we experience life, and when we open up to those experiences, they bring to us the purpose of living; living with aliveness, emotion and consciousness.

I start my book with winter, for it brings to me my most reflective inner journey. It brings to me what I will die to, and I know it will bring me to my rebirthing. So as this book is divided into the four seasons, I hope that my words will speak to you, and bring reason to your personal transitions, deeper understanding to your shifts, and inspiration to your life.

"The chrysalis state of transformation, though appearing to be lifeless like winter, there is still growth underneath."

Winter...

*It all comes full circle—life on the branch, a
tender leaf reaching for its bloom. The leaves
graced with colors of brilliance in their dying,
withering to their falling, trees naked and hollow
in the Winter's wind.*

I START WITH winter because it brings me
to my shedding from all that needs to fall to
the earth of my soul. It's the beginning of an
end, becoming one with my retreating
inward, cocooning, bringing myself to restful
still. I come to embrace the winter. It's longer
nights that bring me to my shadow self. It's a
time to fold in, to examine in the quiet cold;
what it is that needs dying, to let it all go, but
also to rest and ready myself for my opening.
It is often on a winter night under the cold
moon that I hear the still whispering of my
soul to me, bringing me to a place of calm.
Though I quickly tire of winter's embrace, I
know the stirring, the waiting that brings me
to my still centering. It brings me to patience,
taking in this time to rest in my heart. When I
write of winter and it's symbolism with death
and dying, I relate it to what I am dying to

3

myself. I become reflective, silent, and meditative. All that is released in my words brings the pause of the season to one's self in a beautiful way. Even when this shift may be welcoming, or sometimes stifling, it is a time to learn to just be. The chrysalis state of transformation, though appearing to be lifeless like winter, there is still growth underneath.

The winter when I knew my marriage was dying I fractured my ankle. I was in a very still state, unable to do or act. I did not like needing to ask for help or assistance, especially from a partner that was overtly resisting me. I learned during this fragile time of non-movement; it brought me to the still movement of me within. This time of inconvenience was really slowing... bringing me to a dying of a part of me that wasn't me anymore. It was a dying shift I did not accept readily, but it was time that brought me to shed the old, release and let go. This was just the first shift of my long and necessary releasing.

As time went on I would write in my journal, pouring my soul into words as I felt the shift of so much of me falling away. It is often through life's experiencing we feel the falling inward that reach towards who we really are. There has been plenty of time my humanness got in the way; that I almost veered into such depression and felt stuck, lost to my soul. But just as the winter holds the cold in its dying, I held my pain close until it was time to release it.

But you see we don't always release it all at once. We release it in pieces, or sometimes we don't even know yet what it is we need to release. There are many layers of releasing, as there are many things hiding in the shadows of us that need revealing and letting go of. Life has a way of presenting moments that bring you to standstill.

Sometimes if you choose to continue to move fast, keeping busy-ness in your life, you miss what life is trying to teach you. This frequently happens due to commercializing winter holidays, stealing from you the moments to really reflecting within. The true gift of winter is life. Looking back on this past winter and how it kept many of us inside, it was a great opportunity presenting itself, to be still, and go inward. My poems speak of this journey in the winter months, as well as the "winter" months of our lives, which can happen at any time.

Winter brings me closer to my deeper consciousness; I could feel the changes reaching to come out from me. As small animals burrow deep to bring protection to themselves, in the wintertime, we often burrow deep to bring protection to ourselves. You can only stay there for so long though. Staying deep and living in that space of dying can bring you to lifelessness, and not looking at the true beauty of what season you are experiencing.

Winter can cause you to sometimes retreat into your darkness, as its gloom tries to hold you to sadness and make you feel small. But there is still breathing, living movement within you soul, do not let what appears to be lifeless, stop you from your growing. Above all, there is the light and love of life within you, that speaks to you softly, love yourself, embrace yourself, hold yourself in tenderness. This is actually a time of rejuvenation, finding moments that bring you to gratefulness of being. You are still alive, vibrant and growing.

Your winter will begin to thaw. Life will breathe its new seed in you again and it will be time for you to peek your head out and see that life is still breathing, moving, living! The pain you experience through your transitions makes you a stronger and more empowering you. Just when you feel like winter is never going to end, the sun peers down from an iridescent blue sky, and breathes life onto the trees, bringing them to budding, also breathing life into you. Signs of life begin to appear in our outer world, and we begin to feel them within.

My poems about winter reach to touch the darkness, the dying, the letting go and the releasing. They also speak of the tender beauty winter brings from Winter Solstice to the transitions of the full winter moons. Some poems will speak of experiences that happened in the world and how it affected me. When I write about poems of deep suffering they bring an emotional openness to life around me. My hope is always that my words will bring comfort to those who are suffering in a significant way in their journey. What truly affects all of us as we are all connected like the woven roots of a tree.

As you journey through this book, may my words bring an invitation to you to reflect inward, bring ease to whatever you are dying to. May you find renewal of life in your rebirthing, to hang onto the side of your mountain when life is raging against you. Just remember to look up, to see the sun's brilliant face upon you, the sky touching you with a calm blue... always bringing yourself back to you.

November's Closing

November's closing,
comes with a morning-
frosted with winter's whisper.
the sun fills my soul with promise,
with conscious gratitude-
all that has come...
though sometimes in stillness it comes.
our eyes often covered,
with blinders of human choice-
I bring my voice,
a grateful song to sing,
as I come to who I am.
in this moment's bringing,
sometimes when you pull away-
you see how small your suffering,
really is.
I sing again,
a song of humbleness and appreciation.
I become whole over and over.
always coming to my ending,
touching my beginning-
sun sets on my yesterday's steps,
as I now rise to greet new ones.

Winter Stops the Flower Bloom

winter stops the flower's bloom,
to settle in earth-
to rest under,
blanket white.
its bare trees,
reach with fragile arms-
to the chilling wind-
of gray covering my silence.
as this silence comes,
a waiting-
what brings you closing,
you hold yourself in-
a space of conscious stillness.
it is a place to let it all fall down to blend,
into earth's settling-
you lay barren-
ready to be filled,
open to see vision-
rising to see growing.
in this moment of winter's breaking,
healing comes in surrendering-
to the growth of now,
as it comes,
in its own precious time.

Come to My Winter Sun

come to my winter sun,
cold it sits-
in white,
hanging against-
grey skies.
frozen earth,
lays in silent waiting-
for its return.
my heart is still,
longing for its-
returning place,
but inward I return-
where the ground,
of my garden-
awaits its bloom.
I sit as icicles,
form upon my window-
winters settling,
sleeping in quiet rest.
I too sit in winters waiting,
while the holding of
my stillness remains.

December Waits

December waits,
for November's ending-
stillness of white,
against leaves-
blending to earth.
reaching for,
the darkest of days-
calling to us,
time to fold-
resting now,
in the warmth of-
your soul.
time for lessons,
shifts brings your changes,
coming to your,
heart's voice-
whispering in,
the December wind.

it comes through
the trees,
standing,
still,
black,
and naked-
upward reaching-
towards the winter sky.
time for resting,
rejuvenating-
bring you to your cocooning,
to its sheltering,
then birthing-
all of your changing,
to all things new.

Maureen Kwiat Meshenberg

When I Look at the Stars

12/19/12 Children of Sandy Hook Elementary
School.

when I look at the stars,
pinned against the winter sky-
I will take a breath,
and think of you.
when winter white snow flakes,
land on my hands-
I will hold them gently,
and think of you.
when I see the rainbow's,
brilliant hues-
when the wind whispers like music,
when the sweet rain falls-
against my face,
tiny droplets like tears...
I will think of you,
think of you.
for all of life's agony,
there is the miracle of wonder-
bringing thoughts of beauty,
that hold me closer to you.
for you are covering me,
with your presence sweetly-
like angel wings,
I can feel your feathers-
against my cheek,
as I sleep,
and dream of you.

Winter Solstice

winter's breath,
calls in the darkest of nights-
beauty black,
shortness of light.
the sun kisses the stars,
the moon embraces dark-
join now circle of women
our light we now spark.
circle of shes,
we who gather in singing,
bring forth the night-
in our humble existing.
we sing of the barren branch,
the cold winter wind rising-
the darkest of nights,
our intentions now binding.
fire that burns our souls to blend,
the darkest of nights-
will soon slumber and end.
each day will bring us,
to the beauty of light-
ending the longest winter night.
in its dark beauty,
we usher in the light.

December Clothes Me

December clothes me,
in winter-
the silent white,
holds the night,
crisp in stepping-
in its chilling presence.
the air cold in breath,
the winter sky holds the day-
in quietness.
I take the lights,
that decorate my night-
with celebration...
we find warmth by the fire,
hold family near-
this time of year,
in adoration of what this time brings-
hearts that sing in December.
the wind now stings,
as snow gently falls on my window-
sitting, sipping hot chocolate by the tree,
December holds promise in-
the gift it brings,
as I settle in thoughts of giving.

New Moon In January

new moon in January,
falls beneath my sky-
where the breath of night,
swoons the moon-
gently into sight.
the cold still,
melts in-
your presence,
as I whisper-
my longing,
all beholding-
what lays,
exposed-
in my heart.
darkness will not,
betray you-
sliver of light,
return to this-
winter night,
I hold this time-
to my soul,
all that-
completes me,
making me whole.

Maureen Kwiat Meshenberg

Fresh Past the Winter's Dawning

fresh past the winter's dawning,
coming crisp night's morning-
from the frozen wind howling I hear,
in the warmth of my home.
I meditate,
nature's calling-
trees shelter,
the birds still singing.
as the sun slips up,
in the cold blue sky-
glint of fire,
as the day rises.
I again in awe,
of it's restful beauty.
as it wakes and stirs,
the sleeping creatures-
rising with this season,
some still sleep in slumber-
but it stirs me.
I come from my cushion,
warm drink in hand-
warm clothing of comfort,
thanking life,
thanking nature,
thanking being.

Maureen Kwiat Meshenberg

Full Moon Holds January

full moon,
holds January-
in its light,
releasing all that is hard-
often regretful,
into the night,
I do not want regret,
to wane against-
my hoping,
for all that pulls-
me down,
I look up at your gleaming.
light around me,
like a compass-
pulling me out,
of my dark.
what restrains us,
tries to stain us-
the humanness of us,
only wants to speak-
of our guilt.

but my soul rises,
with its howl song-
rises with its dance,
rises in the presence-
of winter's soon retreating.
the moon longs to,
touch the breath-
of the sun,
as I desire to reach-
for the fire,
burning within me-
passion touching,
freeing heart-
beckons me,
to be.

Maureen Kwiat Meshenberg

Let me be my Valentine

let me be my Valentine,
offering love and devotion-
love letters of intentions,
an open invitation-
to embrace myself,
with compassion.
let me be my Valentine,
bring my self flowers-
to breath in the-
fragrance of life,
I will not resist-
but rather insist,
to cover myself-
with grace,
for I am beauty within-
light holds me-
to myself,
I bring love-
to my sacred place,
in my eyes-
as I look in the,
mirror at my face-
I gladly say,
let me be my Valentine.

Maureen Kwiat Meshenberg

When I Dance

For One Billion Rising Dancing to stop violence
against women

when I dance,
I will-
shine,
I will-
shine,
on your dark-
through the crevices,
of your pain-
I will dance.
when I dance,
I will-
shine,
like the-
Valentine moon,
in the winter sky-
reaching towards,
you-
as we meet,
like stars-
in the night,
in brilliance-
against the black,
I will dance.

when I dance,
I will sway-
with my passion,
on this day-,
when my tears,
meet with yours-
with my sisters,
all of the mothers-
all of the daughters,
women together-
we will dance.
bruise to bone,
you are not alone-
one billion stars,
to light your way-
for,
you-
my,
she-
I will dance,
for you today.

Maureen Kwiat Meshenberg

The Cold of Winter

the cold of winter,
has come-
frigid breath,
not holding back-
its howling voice,
ice song-
upon the earth.
frozen melody,
its wailing-
leaving silent rest,
under billows-
of white,
that cling to-
the barren trees.
I hold my candle now,
and look into-
its piercing freeze,
melting through the-
the frozen walls,
that try to pin me-
between memory,
and regret.

I rest now,
on the warmth of-
my breath,
as it leaves me in gentleness.
the heat of my glow,
lets me know-
winter's songs,
will end.
her dance,
will be held-
by the warm,
beating heart-
of life rebirthing,
releasing her sting.

"This is what we experience when coming to the Spring of our souls. We can come out and see the light illuminating its brilliance, and find that we can see the colors of our rainbow bringing the beauty of life and breathe in its amazing moments."

Spring...

In truth, we are all like butterflies.
We all have our beautiful wings;
it's just a matter of time before we spread them
wide and fly.

WINTER IS NOW releasing the chrysalis of me. Movement of bloom is upon me, I feel myself emerging from folding inward, to folding outward, like the flower pushing through snow, to find light and grow. Growing up a Catholic, it was always about Easter... the season of resurrection, Sunday's best dress, patent leather shoes and of course the matching hat and gloves.

As my religious up bringing brought the newness of Spring... of Life... to Christ's life, it was also about the Easter Bunny, blessing baskets, finding Easter Sunday the opening of Spring.

These special memories are held dear to my heart, I hold that time of growing up Catholic as sacred. It brought the rituals of bead praying and prayer altars and the lighting of intentions candles back to my own rituals now. I hold dear the Divine Spirit that resides in me and breathes through me.

This season brings us out of our dreary darkness and into the rebirthing of ourselves again and again. The bloom of our heart's garden is being tilled and ready for flourishing. My poems speak of the opening that comes when we finally shift from our dark and re-enter our light. It is not like the light disappeared, it is always here with us. In this time, we went into our shadow place to go under the deeper layers of our being, to learn about our deeper selves. What was revealed to us in our cocooning is now bringing new and bright understanding to what we have been through. Sometimes it isn't until we have experience the change, that we realize what it was really trying to teach us. We shift from not understanding why to bringing us closer to our compassionate selves.

Every time we experience a transition, it shifts our perspective. We are able to hold others more delicately, we are able to hold the world's ache more compassionately, and we hold ourselves with grace and love as well. I find when I am entering my springtime it is a place of renewing, rejuvenating in ways that I may have not seen clearly before. When the dark of winter is upon us, sometimes the heaviness of gray skies clouds our vision to truly see what life is really offering us. When you see the signs of life emerge in Spring, you begin to see the signs of life in you are emerging... coming to the growth of you.

The thing is, all that we come to learn, and what is brought to our consciousness, was a part of our spiritual nature all along. It is in our humanness we struggle to clearly see what and who we all really are. Through my poems I write of birth, rebirthing, blooming, budding, bursting through our ground. This is what we experience when coming to the Spring of our souls. We can come out and see the light illuminating its brilliance and finding that we can see the colors of our rainbow bringing the beauty of life and breathe in its amazing moments.

Spring as a child, brought the joy of expecting a shift, from death to life, from winter to bloom, seeing the bare naked trees one moment bursting with green the next. A very fond memory was the coloring of Easter eggs with my Dad. We would take our baskets filled with ham, colored eggs, Holy bread, and all that we would eat for our Easter morning breakfast to our church to get blessed. It was a time of honoring the food we get from life the grains, the chicken that lays the eggs, and the nourishment and the growth life offers. We too will see that when we have reached our bloom of life, we are ready to nourish others with our words, our actions, and with our compassionate beauty.

We come to this place of growth quite often in our lives, as our experiences and our journey are constantly changing. The one thing I do know as we cycle like the seasons... when our Spring comes to us, we feel the beauty of our souls within us. Yes indeed, we in truth are like butterflies, let us spread our wings wide now and fly!

The Scent of Spring

the scent of spring,
is calling me-
welcoming sweetness of life,
seed inside me-
ready to bud with newness.
though winter's grasp,
with its still coldness-
its long lifelessness,
for a time-
brought a dying to myself.
death of nature,
a part of my release-
what once belonged to me,
cold ground covering-
now in it's thawing.
change is now coming,
I'm breaking ground,
emerging- like a new season,
light touching love-
love touching grace,
renewing my flourishing-
my nourishment,
of love within.
grateful as the,
rose to sun-
the bird to flight,
the branch to sky...
the scent of spring is calling me,
calling me to life.

Maureen Kwiat Meshenberg

Bud of Life

bud of my life,
tight in closing-
waiting to open,
held nestled enclosed.
acquiescence to my,
unfolding-
the petals now bending,
light pouring through-
the center of my soul.
tenderly I stretch,
pass any resisting-
coming to accepting,
all that completes me.
unfinished, yet,
ready to flourish-
through the newness,
that comes to bring-
me to life once again
as I adapt to all,
that comes to me-

the rising of all that,
rises within me.
it is not the circumstances,
that creates the holding back-
but the fear of pushing through,
to really see,
the flourishing of me exists-
in all that is,
bringing me out of my shadows-
into my day,
the light of me.

Maureen Kwiat Meshenberg

Bloom

bloom,
as spring seeds emerge-
through earth,
poking through-
green reaching towards,
the suns warm rays against blue.
bloom,
that word that brings-
growing,
bringing life-
rebirthing.
bloom,
coming to me,
I see my fields turning-
I see my sky aching,
to push through in bloom.
waking in this moment to see,
my bloom and changes that-
bring me,
to my opening.

The Garden of My Soul

the garden of my soul,
releases my bloom-
my
she,
awaits her-
flowering.
tender rebirth,
of my secret holding-
I lift my heart,
through hands releasing-
open arms wide,
to hold my sky-
awake from my night,
unfolding-
naked from my despair,
naked from my disguise-
clothed in the,
fragrant beauty-
of just me.
rose to thorn,
rain to storm,
sand to desert flower-
I have the power,
to look with eyes-
tenderly,
what wounds me-
heals me,
brings me to my flourishing.

Maureen Kwiat Meshenberg

Journey of The New Moon

journey of my new moon,
new spring-
passing through,
the equinox of change,
it enters my sky-
sliver of light,
through my darkness-
the calling of April,
to new life.
for the power of change,
remains within-
enters the passage way,
of my soul's emerging-
transitioning into,
the light,
of new beginnings-
enters into the,
strength of me.
my intentions,
flying high,
across my-
new moon sky.

the ways of old,
remain sitting-
in winters last hold,
the cold no longer-
takes me,
rising now-
with the new moon,
calling me-
my warm brilliant light,
transforms me to-
let go of,
winter's last embrace.
new moon rises,
in my new spring sky-
brings my truest intentions,
into sight.

Maureen Kwiat Meshenberg

Oh Pink Moon

oh full moon,
pink moon in bloom-
ushering Spring,
on the wind-
she sings,
of life in colorful beginning.
in fullness she rests,
on the dusk sky-
waiting for black,
to hold her light.
she shines on me,
with delight-
gathering my whispering breath,
against her full rising.
I know in the silence,
of my calling-
my dreams to belonging,
like stars that hold her presence-
glitter against black,
in her brilliance.
my reaching for what I now choose,
in my nights watching-
of the pink moon,
I bring my life to living-
and fulfilling,
my desires to truth.

The Creating of Life

open my eyes and see,
the creating of life around me-
seed to birth,
bursting through earth-
its endless breath surrounds me.
from womb,
to the mothers hands-
from forests,
to endless grasslands-
life is creatively unfolding.
even when nature,
or human error pushes back-
the creating of life,
also reacts-
to the strength of it's nurturing,
to the joy of being-
healing to reliving,
coming again and again.
transformation sparks in its,
newness to begin-
creativity in its belonging,
to birth and to live again.

Maureen Kwiat Meshenberg

Rain in my Soul

morning breaks the silence open,
to catch its wandering-
into my soul.
I feel its tender,
reach and fold me-
like a flower,
holding through the storm.
the rain it turns to,
a gentle drizzle,
a flower waiting-
for spring to return,
when I wait on my morning,
with song and singing-
enter in believing,
my opening to its new dawn.
birds that sing,
the song of waking-
I rise with them,
eyes rise with seeing,
words in tender speaking,
ears with listening,
to rain in my soul.
nourishing me,
making me new again.

Bring in my Resurrecting Being

bring in,
my resurrecting being-
unfolding, releasing,
the coming of me-
in the voice that I am,
poetry unleashing.
spilling onto pages,
the words of my believing,
my stories-revealing,
of who I am,
where I am,
and the journey we all take.
starting at my center,
colors moving out,
from me...
like flower petals birthing,
their radiant living to be.
I spill out my colors,
my gift flowing,
onto me,
onto you,
yes unfolding beauty-
life in its giving,
to perpetuate the flow of our lives-
through the words that blend the movement,
my circle of life entering yours.

The Dance of the Monarch Butterfly

blue so iridescent,
so pure in thought-
in longing to be,
my minds eye sees-
through colors,
once so perfect.
my weeping eyes,
hold my own illusions-
they spill out from me,
screaming of the impermanence-
that brings life,
to its breaking.
it all tries to pin me,
between memory-
and regret,
my breath-
holds this space,
that wants to-
take the brilliance,
of life in-
its wanting to,
thrive,

past our arrogance-
and then,
as I watch-
the wings,
colored with hues-
of orange,
traced with-
black lines of beauty,
fluttering wings-
of life upon wind,
upon branch,
upon tree.
their migrating dance,
calls to me-
their lives,
depending upon-
the milkweed.
we transgress,
against-
their purpose,
their thriving-
their surviving,
their wings whisper-

let us dance in the sky,
let us bring life,
to our existence-
to yours,
to the earth.
that we feel,
is as much ours-
as it is,
anyone-
who has any thought,
of compassionate consciousness.
our wings echo,
the past,
the present,
and grasp-
to hang onto,
the future.
fluttering thoughts,
against blue-
so iridescent,
my eyes sting-
against the,
blinding light-
of sun that,

warms wings-
to flight.
I whisper-
to the swallowing,
of the earth-
to its dying,
will we rise-
to plant the seed,
water,
the root,
kiss the stars-
with respecting breath,
and not regret.
plant the milkweed,
in the honoring-
of their flying beauty.

Maureen Kwiat Meshenberg

I Break through Rock

I break through rock,
the side of my mountain-
the nature of me,
nurturing me.
roots that enter,
deep into my waters-
reaching my flowering,
to my skies within.
I thrive through,
my storms-
sometimes,
weathered and worn-
or the seasons,
take my life through-
my rebirth,
but I will not-
be unearthed,
I hold my roots deep-
in my truth,
inside me.

I open to the light,
to the nature of life-
and to those who,
nurture me,
around me.
see me grow,
breaking my ground-
rising up high-
up my climb,
to,
the nature-
of my ever growing life.

Maureen Kwiat Meshenberg

Morning Drenches Me

morning drenches me,
with reassurance-
like a Spring rain,
fields rainbowed with colorful flowers-
that paint it with dance,
if by chance-
I feel empty,
I am filled again-
with life's nourishment.
if I come to feeling extended,
I am drawn back in-
pulled into the center of my soul-
where it begins,
again and again.
to take my overwhelm,
to hold my anxious thoughts-
close in love,
to release them to the blue-
above me like butterflies,
pushing against my wind-
with wings delicate yet strong,
finding their own place-
as I return home to my being,
living life as it is.

Maureen Kwiat Meshenberg

She is Beauty

she is beauty,
filled with grace-
restful bliss,
upon her face-
eyes closed,
dreams of-
passion,
upon green hills-
lined,
with flowers-
that bend,
and sway,
wind swoons her-
to her love song dance.
she is beauty,
filled with light,
that illuminates-
her soul,
holds it-
to her calm.
it is not that-
she has never,
touched pain-
suffering that,
fails her from-

keeping her feet-
pressed firmly,
upon her journey-
her tears,
tender flow-
a river from her,
soul-
she weeps for life,
love,
loss,
her dreams.
she is beauty,
holding
her world,
with love,
she sings
with beauty,
in laughter,
in melancholy,
holding her truth-
instinctually,
she is you-
she is me.

Maureen Kwiat Meshenberg

Flower Moon

Flower Moon,
through trees in full bloom,
I stand in front of your open gaze,
into dark that hangs-
calling in my summer.
Flower Moon,
May now exits-
calling in June,
I see your glistening,
call to my releasing-
bringing life to my journey,
calling me home.
For if I sit under your glowing,
I find in my knowing,
I am ready to begin,
what folds out,
now folds in,
to the light of your blossoming,
oh, Flower Moon.

Maureen Kwiat Meshenberg

"I am sun reaching,

**I am plant to earth growing,
bird to sky flying,
I am my eyes beholding the clouds
that grace blue.**

Summer...

*I rest upon lazy in a meadow full of daisies that
hold their petals easy towards the day. Summer
time always reminds me to be playful as a child.*

I HAVE SO many fond childhood memories,
I must admit, I am grateful for the time I was
born. Today is so filled with its technology,
kids texting each other, or just using social
media as a means to communicate, saddens
my heart. To not experience the fun of just
sitting lazily in a field of grass talking with a
group of friends, I hope some kids take that
opportunity to do so.

Growing up in summer meant running
through sprinklers, drinking from the garden
hose, climbing trees. I didn't have a cell
phone to call my best friend, I just yelled her
name up at her bedroom window to come out
and play. We were outside all day, until it
turned dark outside. Summer time I always
associate with playtime, connecting to the
brightness of the Summer sun's heat and
enjoying every minute of it. To me it is the
season to bring out your inner child, find

your beautiful moments in nature as they spontaneously explode with colors just like fireworks on the 4th of July. This is a time of movement, action, taking off in flight in love and adventure. My own childhood adventures, and those when my children were young are my fondest summer memories.

Until recently, I found it very difficult to enjoy my summers, for it has been during the past three summers I experienced such a tremendous upheaval and unwanted shifts in my life. Summer of 2010 was especially difficult, hearing the words from my husband stating that he no longer loved me, devastated me to the core. Also, during the Summer of 2010, I experience a horrific event during a tornado like storm while huddling in our basement stairwell with my two teenage sons. A huge tree came crashing through our home, leaving huge gaping holes in our roof making it rain inside our house. The whole devastation and wreckage it left, mirrored what was happening to my marriage. It was surreal. In the Fall of 2010 we tried to salvage our marriage only for me to feel his constant distain of staying with me, until the summer of 2011 I finally had the courage to say, "You have cut the cord of our bond, I can no longer live this way any more." From 2011-2014 we remained separated, and again in the Summertime of 2014, I experienced what its like to be served with divorce papers. Coming to a final ending in this over 20-year relationship in my life, has been one of the greatest shift in my life. I have experienced the death of my parents, but this was something I did not expect.

As much as all this pains me and seems to put a damper on my Summer, I wrote a poem called "The Final Ending". It talks about :

> the final embrace,
> and letting your arms-
> slip to your side,
> watching it leave you-
> floating pass the sky,
> behind you.
> the bridge between,
> this gap I see-
> my loss of life,
> and my new beginning,
> the light holds,
> a tender beam-
> towards my path of,
> healing.
> as behind me,
> the bridge fades away-
> into a sunset,
> full of yesterdays.

Just as life is bringing this ending to my life, I am embracing so many new beginnings. I was recently published in Catherine Ghosh's Anthology: *Journey of the Heart: An Anthology of Spiritual Poetry by Women*. I have been having doors open up to many other writing projects, bringing me delightful beginnings to me as a Poet. This is my joy, my Summer, my time to shine. I find that even though my human fragility wants to shut out Summer, I find myself breathing in nature's calling for me to enjoy her beauty and her sweet embrace.

I have been having the pleasure of going to a favorite spot of mine in Wheaton, Illinois at the Theosophical Society. There they have a magnificent labyrinth that I have enjoyed walking to moving meditation. There is a pond with Willows that billow and touch the earth. I sit there and write and bring myself to the present, enjoying the moments of summer's gentle holding. So I try to release what I think what summer reminds me of, holding onto the newness and freshness it brings. I also find summer especially enjoyable during the Full moons. To be able to go out on a warm summer night and behold the Full Super Moon brings great delight to my soul. You will find my poems, bringing in her beauty, fragrance and powerful Full moons to call Summer into your souls.

I will continue to hold onto my childhood memories and memories with my children, and the moments I bring to my summer now. To allow this sweet season to embrace me in beauty and in warmth, I hope my poems will embrace you in beauty and warmth as well.

Maureen Kwiat Meshenberg

Ascendance of Light ~ Summer Solstice

ascendance of light,
warms our summer sky-
rising of brightness,
clothing the day-
with delight,
opens with illumination-
we gather in celebration,
of the flowering of the sun's-
full bloom.
resting so high,
kissing the night-
with the fragrance,
of fire-
we gather our desires,
as they burst-
from our souls,
dancing.
we bring this longest day,
our attention and remember-
summer brings out-
the chance to take,
the pleasures of warmth and laughter-
celebrating the season,
with exuberance.

Maureen Kwiat Meshenberg

I Rest Upon Lazy

I rest upon lazy,
in a meadow-
full of daisies,
that hold their-
petals easy,
towards the day.
I rest upon summer,
because she covers-
me with clover,
and green,
and trees,
and heat that-
spills sweat upon,
my face-
the dancing rain,
washes it all away-
as I rest-
upon green,
upon today.

ready to embrace-
what comes today,
brings you to steady-
and to strength,
beyond measuring it,
through your mind's eye-
for what holds you,
can not be uttered-
with your mind's voice,
only from within-
your soul,
brings you to the-
wholeness you already are.
let the scars lay,
let fear crouch away-
for the she inside of you-
is here to stay.

Maureen Kwiat Meshenberg

I am Sun Reaching

I am sun reaching,
I am plant to earth growing-
bird to sky flying,
I am my eyes-
beholding,
the clouds that-
grace blue,
white mist of just being-
floating,
being me-
feather like,
whispering to my connecting...
I feel its mystery,
touching my soul-
I am with all that is life,
we are connected by light-
brings us to our,
touching each others longing.
let me always be,
in my awakening to see,
to connect,
embrace and be-
in all of these...
I am truth,
breaking through-
soil to tree,
earth to sea,
you to me.

Maureen Kwiat Meshenberg

New Moon Resting in the Summer Sky

new moon,
that sits-
like a sliver slit,
tilting against night-
my soul holds,
what wants to burst-
from me,
to be me,
in the moment of-
my light.
coming in my,
stillness-
what surges from,
my being,
what weighs upon-
my soul and holds,
me close.
today just once,
forget about whats-
supposed to be,
and just be.

to all that now stand,
upon their path gazing-
towards the stars,
that embrace-
the new moon,
rising in summer's resting.
we with purpose, hope,
longing…
pulling back broken,
but lifting it out-
as intentions,
to the distant sky-
setting us free.
in our moment,
of returning-
our souls,
to just being,
to just breathing.

Maureen Kwiat Meshenberg

Rose Moon Rises

rose moon rises,
crosses over-
the summer night,
June calls,
to the opening-
of her flowering,
resting on summer's breath.
waiting in surrendering,
what brings me to-
her beauty holding,
the warm sky.
what brings me to-
her swelling color,
as the dark sparks-
her light upon me,
so full,
in her bright returning,
the stars sway in her-
glowing,
bringing my heart whispers-
to the calling of the moon song.
I rise,
I stand-
heart open,
lifted hands-
just like her rose blooming,
in the June sky.

Unfolding from the Eastern Sky

unfolding from the Eastern sky,
clouds that hold the sun-
layering on each other,
resting on blue.
the sun peers through,
veils of white-
to bring it's light upon me.
I look up,
not only to notice morning,
but holding its waking close to me.
summer waits not,
for the seer to notice her rising-
but it is there-
because it is becoming day,
just being,
what it brings every day-
through its natural existing.
as it shows me-
a glimpse of her presence,
and I breathe summer in.

Maureen Kwiat Meshenberg

Mid-Summer's Waking

Summer's waking,
I caught a glimpse -
of my shadow,
against the summer nights taking-
a few moments I lie awake.
I see why I hold,
close to the stillness-
and the warmth of its calling,
and yet,
could it be,
that I fold in-
like a leaf,
that is done-
colors dispersing,
bleeding into dying-
to my frailties,
only to be exposed-
to my aching.
what am I bringing to,
my lights glowing-
do I choose who it touches,
does the sun choose-
who to shine on?

I can fold,
and open-
and reach bloom again,
as summer shifts-
and settles with opening,
my soul responds,
to all I am.
break me open,
to be filled again-
like a summer rain,
hitting dry land-
absorbed in my soul,
refreshing waves-
of movement,
bringing me-
to my flow.

Maureen Kwiat Meshenberg

Fire and Light

when I bring my thoughts to resting,
let quiet hold my mind-
summer song sings to me,
through the wind inside,
of me...
I take myself walking-
see the flowers reach to sun.
I open with the beauty around me-
while the warm suns heat,
colors my sky-
fire and light-
brings in the summer night.
the dark speaks of the stars-
as the evening thunders
with rain,
echoing, they will be out
to play with the clouds again.
to all that I listen to and see,
bringing it all to me-
to hold in its,
full breathtaking moment-
is to let quiet guide me-
to my soul embracing-
conscious thankfulness.

Maureen Kwiat Meshenberg

When Sorrow so Deep

when sorrow,
so deep-
takes your soul,
you're lost-
to your grief,
know that today-
holds a promise,
of believing.
when you hold,
into sight-
on what you,
truly see-
when joy and sorrow,
blends,
brings you back to,
whole again.
is when you hold,
life simple-
in your hands,

like a child –
that holds,
a firefly-
watching it light,
a warm summer sky.
the glow of,
your soul knows-
hope is there,
when love holds-
you close,
you return to-
your place,
that brings to you-
your grounding peace.

Maureen Kwiat Meshenberg

Super Thunder Moon

rain that covers her sky,
with a thousand tears falling-
spiraling down,
touching earth-
clouds that lay,
soft and gray-
covering her face,
as her brilliant stream-
of light,
still holds the night sky-
with her fullness.
though across the universe,
your gleam-
may reach with shine,
upon others with perfect radiance-
thunder,
dancing drums rumbling-
play their beating song,
revealing their power-
in the sky.
oh moon,
super thunder moon-
not that you are hiding,
behind the storming sky.

you are there,
peering through the dark-
even my shadows,
that cover my gleam-
of me,
bring up my-
deep rooted intentions,
pulled up-
by trembling hands,
I who stand-
at summer's gate,
and wait-
for your illumination.
I come,
with arms held high-
cup the rain,
in my hands,
water healing-
flowing down,
and through me.
super moon,
you are here,
I capture your radiance,
pass the raging sky-
capturing your perfect light,
into my heart.

Maureen Kwiat Meshenberg

Summer's Coming Near its Last Refrain

summer's coming,
near its last refrain-
rain soaks,
the
earth,
as it drinks it in-
still bringing,
the fragrant beauty-
of daffodils,
lined up-
like little suns,
dancing on green.
near a resting pond,
where a heron-
stands within her stillness,
we both gaze amongst-
the willows,
that drop down-
billowing outward,
tenderly kissing-
the earth.
I feel summer's,
sweet heat-
holding us in this day-

as I rise to,
walk the labyrinth,
moving meditation-
as the trees sing,
summer's song.
still in its lush blooming,
still holding-
wanting me to see,
summer's moment for me,
trees still so-
full of green,
soon to embrace-
transitions,
colors falling-
upon my rising.
I embrace,
summer's last refrain-
as in my stillness,
I watch-
the morning rain.

Maureen Kwiat Meshenberg

I Saw Summer's Hold

I saw Summer's hold,
her heat tenaciously-
fell upon my exhaustion.
though lovely in her bloom,
her exit is welcomed...
because the chill of Fall,
calls me-
as painted leaves,
float through my mind-
I catch them,
as promises of change.
I hold the wet,
the chill grey of autumn's calling-
for me to open...
releasing the colors of my life-
that no longer belong to me,
the death of my belonging comes,
like dancing leaves in the wind.

"I am sun reaching, I am plant to earth growing, bird to sky flying, I am my eyes beholding the clouds that grace blue."

Autumn...

*Rest on leaves that cover earth blending colors that
fold, touching autumn's breath.
When the trees transition with colors kissed with
red; hues of orange and yellow;
crisp air ushering summer's refrain, I embrace this
season like no other.*

AUTUMN IS MY absolute favorite season. The nature of this season brings me to holding the changes and shifts of summer, bringing in the harvesting of me. I collect all the things I have learned and hold so dear, and bring my gratitude into this season. I love dressing my house in Autumn and also love the hauntingly playfulness of Halloween. I celebrate my birthday in Autumn with my identical sister Marianne... in November. We celebrate it usually in a nature way. We often go horseback riding, hiking in leaves on the River walk and find ourselves enjoying the day clothed in Autumn colors.

During this time, I find myself preparing to shift into winter, but also take time to enjoy the brilliant shifts of this season.

Though in beauty the trees are dying, becoming bare, to rest in winter, I hold this time with awe and adoration for this season.

Raising my children during Autumn was filled with walks in nature, the crunching of leaves under our feet. I would take my children to pumpkin patch farms where they would go on horse drawn hayrides, feed goats and chicks, and run through cornstalk mazes, after which I would joyfully purchase pumpkins for us to carve or paint. Dressing up our house for Halloween was especially exciting as each year my children dreamed what they would dress up as and look forward to trick or treating. It would often involve a trip to my father's house, where their "Papa" would have a special treat bag for them. Thanksgiving was also very special, time for family, grateful for the food we have and for the gathering of memories of this special time.

The shifts of this season bring a closing of all that is colorful; holding the last breath of summer until it embraces the chill wind of the upcoming season. In my poems I speak of the beauty of nature during this time, even though it releases beauty only to be clothed in dying. I find myself coming to a place of dying, and letting go. Layers upon layers, I eventually find the releasing of me. I am like the leaves of an oak tree falling tenderly to the ground of my heart. I find this time of letting go sometimes difficult, but at the same time grateful, for what life has brought to me this far. This is a time to for me to get ready to move into standstill. This does not mean there is no movement, for me it becomes inward movement. I am getting to go inward and find my resting to go deep and find my aloneness within. This does not mean being lonely, it means finding comfort and being able to embrace being alone with myself. When you allow yourself to shift into being comfortable alone, you are accepting you for who you are; this is accomplishing a great shift.

Think about how the trees were once so lush and green and full of life. Then they burst into brilliant colors, only to have them fall away; to stand naked and bare against the winter wind and grey skies. They still hold themselves as trees. They do not cower away from themselves but stand strong and tall... awaiting the birthing of their green again. We are like trees and just as the songbird perches on their branch in all the seasons, so do we have the song of our souls embracing us. We can accept ourselves in our nakedness, our blooming, our brilliance, and our aloneness. It is a time to fold into gentle tenderness and compassion towards ourselves. To find the shifts of the colors of you, all that dies is re-birthed again.

Let this season stand strong and vibrant in your heart, hold the true colors of you close, so when your winter comes, you can take a piece of those colors and hold them close to your soul. May my poems of Autumn brings its beauty to your heart as you embrace this season and find its tender holding.

I Come to September's Calling

I come to September's Calling,
in my unease-
I go to my place-
deep inside,
bending within,
the longing-
of my soul,
pulls me through,
my surrendering.
seeing the shifting season
ahead,
for my harvest is ready-
what comes to
empty,
will be filled-
again.
with open hands-
tenderly reaching,
towards the colors-
that blends into,
the coming-
of the new me.
again,
and again,
I will find-
the rebirthing,
of my soul

Maureen Kwiat Meshenberg

Find Your Time to Settle

find your time to settle,
pull into your resting place-
gather to relaxation,
smell the chilled rain-
on a September morning.
find your time to take ease,
bend to your quiet place,
a time to rein in,
your running-
sometimes caught,
into rushing-
that you miss hearing,
the gentle voice within.
quietly,
breathe-
in,
now it is time,
to exhale with-
sweet calm within you,
take kindness and gentleness-
to your doorstep,
come to the nourishing-
of your soul.

I Come to Autumn

come to Autumn,
as she beckons us-
to stay still with her,
in her changing presence.
let her bring a grateful song,
to my soul-
I come to her-
with appreciation with what,
she brings to us...
the abundance of all that is,
life... death... life...
but in these changes,
that come again and again,
impermanence brings us-
to our finding.
we ourselves,
our risings-
our fallings.
like the golden sun rising,
on an autumn morning-
like leaves falling delicately,
on a brisk October day.
this is the way with nature,
this is the way of our souls.

October

October,
you come with your-
yielding harvest,
gathering abundance,
then releasing...
all in October's last breath,
of summer departing-
the cold wind bring the colors,
settling into winter's kiss.
do not let the chill disturb you,
comfort & change wraps,
its warmth around you.
cocooned to life's molding,
you are coming to new beginnings-
even in dying,
life begins.

Autumn's Dawning

In this day,
in this morning-
I clothed my soul,
with autumn's dawning.
transitioning colors,
to fabric me-
resting to be,
so freely-
touching my life,
with possibilities.
for in this breath of change,
that comes to my morning-
seasons outside,
comes to me with beauty-
I choose how it holds me,
to wrap around me.
breathe into my waking,
I see my shifting-
to opening-
the spilling out of me,
are my colors
to just be me.

Maureen Kwiat Meshenberg

The Leaves Have Come Out Now

the leaves have come out now,
with their brilliant dance-
through dying celebration,
they rise with the wind,
to the open sky.
branches held high,
splendor touching sun-
the day has just begun,
path lays a carpet-
of colors for me,
path of my calling-
rejoices with the season,
even in dying beauty.
sweet harvest has come,
to my soul,
the deep moon will rise-
to cover the sky,
over dark blue night.
it will rest easy-
with the season of dying beauty,
through death life births its brilliance-
with radiant hues of living.

Autumn Hunter's Moon

Autumn Hunter's moon,
dusts summer off-
its midnight sky,
your light rests-
on the full gleam of the
seasons shifting.
in quiet resting,
the seeds are gathered,
the trees surrender-
soon becoming,
bare arms stretching,
touching your shining-
in the chill calm of darkness.
you hold the evening's beauty,
capturing our intentions,
drawing them into,
your still waiting.
darkness folds,
the cold-
now holding,
the orange breath of sunset-
as the sky slips behind black.
your glow holds until,
dawn touches your fading-
as we release our opening,
to your reflecting.

Maureen Kwiat Meshenberg

Rest on Leaves

rest on leaves.
that cover earth,
blending,
colors that
fold,
touching autumn's breath.
it comes with a turning,
my life not exerting-
a stillness upon me,
to settle within.
listen to the season's
hum upon the wind,
ushering a chill,
a silence to its closing,
trees now release
their garments,
now flowing
colors,
stand tall and naked-
against the dark sky

like me,
I shed
to release,
to pause and see-
the resting of me.
it brings me to listening,
to changes beginning,
in the shifts now-
splitting,
ending
coming,
opening
to myself seeing,
the season of me.

Maureen Kwiat Meshenberg

October Has Settled

October has settled,
outside my window-
wind's rhythm,
now in tune with Autumn's chill.
trees sway to the breeze,
as falling leaves-
land on dampened soil.
darkening my sky,
days grow shorter-
clouds play tag with the sun.
oh October,
you rise up in me-
as I gratefully,
welcome your song.
seasons of my soul,
scattered then whole-
like leaves that wither,
on October's ground.
all will rebirth again...
bringing forth life-
at my winter's end.

October Saturday

October Saturday finds me,
sun clothes me-
in the song that I give-
to her,
penetrating through me,
melody of my heart.
awakening with the sun,
glistening on chilled leaves-
of autumn dancing-
in the winds of,
an October sky-
I wander to the,
sky inside me-
past my mistaking,
of yesterday-
past my resisting,
let it all be soothed-
by the warmth that swells,
and melts it all away-
willingness to be-
I with my Saturday,
my Saturday with me.

Maureen Kwiat Meshenberg

Harvest Moon

whisper to my soul to hush now,
I feel the pull of your light-
drawing my soul,
gathering it all-
like baskets full of
my harvesting,
growing,
rebirthing,
now dying,
as the
tireless trees,
leaves now turning
amber,
golden kissed
with
red-
now ready to rest.
I slip quietly,
go to my deep calm.
feel the moon rising-
above my darkness.

I wait upon the movement,
for my rising inside me-
stirring me to call upon all that I name,
all that I want to be-
to be nothing less,
but everything more-
all that matters,
all that is true-
all that is my "she".
no sound is murmured,
only my breath-
my inner voice,
waiting, wanting, learning, belonging...
as I am taken to my silence,
the moon washes me in pure light-
oh Harvest Moon,
bringing in my season of change.

Maureen Kwiat Meshenberg

I Gather Leaves

I gather the leaves,
that lay softly to earth-
colors fading,
brown upon water-
drifting,
in quiet rest.
life gathers,
my changes-
slowly they come,
the dying of my
wanting,
turning my
will towards
allowing.
it all
blends-
in the end,
empty,
full,
closed,
now open.
I gather in,
the season-
my soul now,
reaching for-
release.

November Greets Us

November greets us,
touches the dawning-
of Winter's calling,
still hold Autumn close-
leaves that shift,
from splendor-
to surrender,
to stillness-
float delicately,
from the solemn trees,
to earth's embrace.
as I shed,
myself-
entering,
my soul's embrace,
changes that calls-
to my dying,
to rebirthing again-
leaning into,
November's greeting-
it teaches me,
the surrendering of me.

Maureen Kwiat Meshenberg

Dances Upon Leaves of November

she dances with ease,
upon the leaves-
of November,
finding her colors-
blend into earth-
she dances as she pleases,
without caring who
sees her,
she follows the steps-
and makes them her-own.
twirling with the winds,
of change-
grateful for,
the song she sang,
just a melody-
to coax her steps,
moving to the shifts,
that haven't happen-
yet,
but she is ready to dance-
to the season of her heart-
drum beating-
rhythm seeking,
ready to take part-
in the soul dance,
of her life.

Thanksgiving is Here

come gather round the table,
with family and with friends-
come gather round the table-
together breaking bread.
grateful for the bounty,
of food laid on the table-
grateful for the working hands,
and bodies that are able.
grateful for the eyes to see,
delicious aromas for us to smell-
conversations within us swell-
with joyful memories,
the years,
that bring our stories.
it all comes down to matters,
of the heart-
those still here,
those who have departed.
yes, it is in gathering,
that we hold all dear-
whether they live far,
or whether they are near,
giving thanks,
lifting our glasses, say cheers,
Good Day-
Thanksgiving is here.

The Seasons of Life

the seasons of life,
draw my breath of inspiration-
the movement of their beauty,
brings me to contemplation.
to view them as signs,
of wonder and lessons-
bringing their stories-
oh these wondrous seasons.
summer's light, bursting with life-
flourishing sweetness,
heat of my morning.
flowing into the trees,
now folding into colors of earth-
letting go of their birth,
dying into beauty.
ushers in the cold,
the first fall of silent snow-
winter's night gives rest,
soul cocooning, time of growing, within...
naked trees reach toward the sky,
green becomes release-
brings earth's birthing,
spring enters with life.
always assuring me,
with the hope of the seasons,
as they unfold me inside,
movement of inspiration.

The poet's journey could well be said to be a long one... as long as there is passion for life, there are words to pen. Thus it is for Maureen—as she wraps up the path of a debut author and brings the fruit of poetry to readers, she is at once inspired to begin anew, with the second in her series—

The Kindle version of this book is available: http://www.amazon.com/dp/B00P9F8U62

The privilege of writing a review for the benefit of other readers can be easily achieved here: http://bit.ly/SeasonsReview

The She Within, to be released in 2015.

Maureen Kwiat Meshenberg

www.ingramcontent.com/pod-product-compliance
Lightning Source LLC
LaVergne TN
LVHW021510080426
835509LV00018B/2468